T0197253

The Principles of

Adeatology

365 plus one nuggets for daily fulfillment and successful living

Trafford rev. 08/03/2011

 www.trafford.com

North America & international
toll-free: 1 888 232 4444 (USA & Canada)
phone: 250 383 6864 ♦ fax: 812 355 4082

This book is dedicated to the word that was in the beginning.

Great words of wisdom, tonic for a great life!
These are 366 terrific, edifying and highly encouraging motivational words of wisdom. Encapsulated, packaged in adequate doses for daily tonic, the principles of Bankole Adeate termed Adeatology are recommended for daily motivational needs. The author's meteoric rise is a clear demonstration that these principles are indeed dependable as a catalyst for a life of success. These are indeed modernized, compressed and re-orientated proverbial expressions.

Ambassador Lawrence Obisakin
Author, Pastor and Minister Permanent Mission of Nigeria to the United Nations, United States

Refreshingly different and destined to go places!

Mrs Gloria Essien- Danner
Executive Director, GM Public and Government Affairs, EXXON Mobil Affiliates in Nigeria,

Bankole Adeate has taken his place among the wise by giving us *The Principles of Adeatology.* The book is a compilation of what can rightly be described as "Sayings of the Wise" or "Words of Wisdom". He has also been generous by giving us one for each day of the year. Reading through the book reminds me of the writings of Rudyard Kipling or more recent inspirational writers like ZigZiglar. We need more of these inspirational books from African writers!
Professor Clement Bewaji
Director, Ambassadors Speakers Club International,
University of Ilorin, Nigeria.

This meticulously handled collection of 366 thought – provoking wise sayings by Bankole Adeate is highly commendable work. Not only are the sayings spiritually uplifting, they are applicable to everyday life. It is a compulsory reading for anyone who wants to enjoy everydaylife. Bankole's simple, easily comprehensible and fluent style of writing is impressive. It makes the book easy to read for all age groups. It is indeed a book for every season-a thought each day for every leap year. Great!!!

Mr Dotun Adepoju,
A Senior Nigerian diplomat, Budapest, Hungary

The book, *The Principles of Adeatology,* is a compilation of 366 inspirational and reflective statements that are food for thought. Some of the statements would definitely be familiar to readers; many others, however, would hit us with the freshness of dawn that gives promise of a new awakening. The author, without doubt, offers us divinely inspired virtues borne out of years of profound observation, myriads of experiences and personal reflections.
I strongly believe that if you can reflect on one statement per day, you are bound to bask in exceeding joy and success all through the year. They are thought provoking. Enjoy as you read.

Dayo Ogunbekun PhD
AGM, Technology Department, GTBank, Nigeria

Introduction

The Principles of Adeatology represents concepts and ideologies mentally formed from my meditation and thoughts; and largely powered by divine inspiration. They are powerful reflections and sometimes rhetorical questions extending from applying knowledge to the conscious and subconscious situation and circumstances of life.

The words inscribed in these nuggets are fundamentals, distinct, and personal. Some of the messages may be familiar as veritable obligations and requirements for us to live right; they should, however, be embraced into our subconscious as an eternal guide for attaining good success and for achieving personal fulfillment.

These divinely inspired nuggets are guaranteed to live on in your memory, guide you through the paths that are invisible to the human eyes; and lead you even when other hands let go of you.

To bring it closer, let me simply say that some of these principles possess general ingredients for the needs of all, while many others possess specific instruments for your individual and specific needs. As you unlock the door of the Principles of Adeatology, you will realize that many of the nuggets will transpose you into a world where words are used as bricks in constructing monumental sky scrapers and gigantic buildings whose foundations are laid with the costliest of gems!

The 366 nuggets in this book offer some relief in your frantic search for knowledge and your earnest race after wisdom. It does not matter what your dreams are taking you through, or where your dream is leading you; starting from this moment, the principles of adeatology will definitely get you to your desired destination.

001

*F*riend! You are the end product of the
choices you make. Your present situation
speaks of the decision you made some time ago.
Let your thoughts be deep and your decisions
unblemished. Always remember that rash
decisions will end you up rashly in the trash!

002

*W*hen the issues of this life like the ocean roars
at you, and the realities of your circumstances
like the river barks and the streams of your failures
threaten so hard, soar with your dreams above the
storm, be true to what you believe in, holding your
breath, never giving up, until you behold and see the
fall of the wicked, and the resurgence of the great!

003

The greatest battle any individual can win is the one won in the war field of the mind. If you can overcome here; you can overcome all the way. Guard your heart with all you have got; when the enemy takes over your HEART every other thing in your possession will likely fall apart!

004

When men shower praises on you for your victory; refer them to your God who knows all about your story; lay all your trophies at his feet! The temporal presence of satisfactory progress and peace of mind should not be celebrated as eternal bliss. You need to check yourself when everything seems fine... my friend, that's when you need to watch!

005

Someone said, "as far as your eyes can see will determine how far your dreams can be". I disagree, because as far as your mind can conceive, your heart can believe and much farther can your dreams take you. So throw your body behind yourself and let loose all you've got - your mind, your brain - and the whole of you will follow!

006

You really have nothing to lose, by being positive about other people. You may think you are always right when you see things through your own eyes. But sometimes, we need to look through the mirror, through others' eyes; they may be right as well.

007

Maybe I woke up on the wrong side of the bed, I was so hungry and was almost looking for anything to eat, I mean anything, and then I remembered that the easiest way not to feel hunger is not to eat anything at all. There is a lesson to learn in everything that happens; observe and analyze the situation, it can never be a coincidence

008

Pursue your dream with vigour and grit, with verve and determination. You are merely having fun. Anything that will assist you to get to your dream land will give you the greatest satisfaction you ever desired. Never loose sight of the shore, though in the middle of the raging sea. Align your telescope, re navigate; you can only determine the course!

009

I have never heard or seen any bird flying up there in the sky colliding with other birds, or fighting in the sky and crashing with a long fall to the ground. The sky up there, where the greats are assembled, has wide enough space for everyone to fly. But I have seen and heard of a man, who will do everything humanly possible to pull down a fellow man from the height of peace and glory; even though the earth is saturated with limitless opportunities for everyone. Learn to pull other people up; learn to help others succeed; live to give your all and assist someone to climb the ladder that will lead to their greatness. Utilize the space of the earth freely without rancor. Let's start helping, let's start assisting, let's start giving, let's start offering, and let's start serving; for the choices you're making today will open wider doors of opportunities enough for your heart desires.

010

I'm puzzled by this... when Monday morning comes, Friday night is just like the tick of a clock, and it seems everything is heading somewhere! As the nights roll out and the new day dawns, the hours required to achieve what you're destined to attain, to arrive where you're destined to be, to overcome the heights you are determined to climb are fiercely reduced. There is no time to lag behind.

011

*H*ear some of our ambitions then; "I want to become the best musician in the world..." "I want to become a Pilot..." "I want to become a Medical doctor, even to the extent of treating fallen soldiers during earth breaking wars..." "I want to become a Lawyer..." "I want to become the President..." "I want to become this and that..." Hmmm, what happen to all of those dreams? Have we forgotten them? Dreams are like whispers from the night, they have hands that beckon and sometime they signal at us, yet they are invincible. We nurture them when our hearts were still tender, but now... what happen to those dreams? Don't kill your dreams; live it!

012

*S*o many disappointments may have often triggered the question: Do I have a dream? Never leave it halfway; what you know would give you the greatest joy you eagerly desired. Completion is the key to successful satisfaction. Do you know that the world was once barren and desolate? Men explored and improved on it. Would you leave the world a better place than you met it? Truth is, as long as you have a brain, you have a dream.

013

Some people are living the script written by someone else. Why don't you write your own script, why not live your own life? Be you! It is indeed a tragedy of life that many of us wrote down great goals, but ended up pursuing other people's goals. You never really will be happy if all you did was live other people's dreams.

014

You know what dreams does? It awakens you in the thick of the night. It makes you work harder. True dream brings out the best in you. As far as my eyes can see, I have never seen any great man or woman with two heads. Either have I seen any man or woman, who will not achieve what he or she resolves to achieve as long as he or she exerts all of his or her effort!

015

What legacy will you leave behind when your transit visa on earth expires? Are you building your life everyday on the platform of excellence? No matter how little, no matter how trivial, no matter how negligible; contribute something, excellent, to the ecosystem, to human beings, to the land, to the sea, to your family, to your colleagues, to your country, to the world - that you may be remembered like Shakespeare.

016

People who think they are up there, always ignore the little who are down in the food chain, they quickly forget that the little pieces of clothes make the style fit for wearing. The strong is not recognized by the smaller people he bullied and oppressed, rather he is measured by how he strengthened the weaker people.

017

You will have to deny yourself some pleasures of life to make sure you obtain the treasures of this life. Get the treasures first and the pleasure will follow. You may lose the treasure though, if pleasure takes charge of your life.

018

One of the greatest words ever heard and ever spoken by a MAN, but hardly practiced be men is FORGIVENESS. You probably still keeping a grudge that the other person has no slightest idea. Move on! Forgive! You also have been forgiven before. Forgiveness is the invisible thread that binds, like an aromatic balm, if when rubbed on time, would heal the worst pain of them all!

019

I knew a man who lived his life fighting for other people, he died even at 71, having fought so hard, a battle I tagged, "piercing through the earth", he fought for others and forgot to fight for himself, little did I know that when you stand in the gap for others, the gap will be full, such that you don't need anyone to stand in the gap for you because the gap is already occupied by people waiting to fight on your behalf.

020

I t's never too late or too early to pursue your dreams. If you decide not to take that step, hundreds of people are waiting out there hoping you would not. Act right! You are never too young to dream, nor too old to have dreams. It's never too late to pursue your dream! You count for nothing if you have no dream to fulfill.

021

T here are two things that separate everyone's aspirations; you can either be a source of inspiration or a symbol of desperation. You have been inspired by people around you and in distance, the books you read and the nature you see. Has someone been inspired by you? Resolve to inspire your generation; your seed of inspiration sowed would be harvested in future generations!

022

If you wish to be more than what you are today; if
you wish to be great at what you do now; you need
to know how great people stayed on top. The secret
can be found in the strength of their mind, followed
closely by discipline, determination and enthusiasm.
They never let go the cords of principles that bind
them to their success ends! What it takes to be number
one, to remain number one and even outlast your
position under intense pressure and stiff completion –
it takes humility, consistent hard work and the fear of
God.

023

Three things control everything on planet earth ...
wisdom, power and wealth; what I called the wPw
compendium. What you know, will either make or
mar you, likewise what you don't know, would most
likely follow the same pattern. Know what to know!
Interestingly everyone has the wPw compendium
inborn, inherited or imbibed!

024

Regardless of the circumstances and the
forgetfulness that may trail your mood; don't
ever give up on your dreams. Follow your truth stint.
The roughest road oftentimes goes straight to the
top of the tallest mountains, Mount Everest, Mount
Kilimanjaro, and many others. How rough is the road
you're treading today? Remain focused no matter
how steep the road is, you shall fulfill your destiny.

025

*I*n my meditation, I discovered something, and I think I should share it, I naturally accept that living things (human, animal, trees) are the only creatures that speak and understand their types, suddenly I realize a mysterious truth that non-living things, stone, sand, sea, moon, stars, earth, etc all speak and understand themselves too. Then you can speak and give command to any of these and they will answer, because you are created to dominate them. Start speaking your way into greatness, accomplishments and achievements.

026

*W*eigh your actions, you never know when and how it could affect you or someone else, today, tomorrow or sometime in the future. Is it better not to show up, than arrive late? The habit of getting there on time and being ready before time is a virtue that sets us before kings. Subject yourself with the readiness to arrive earlier than scheduled.

027

*B*attles are fought; battles are won. Losers are countless, winners are rare, but those who fight on their knees in prayer earn victory long ahead of others. Pray without ceasing! Great victory in the history of mankind, are not achieved with sophisticated weapons; but rather they are won on bended knees!

028

When we expend our energy on things that will add little value to our lives, we are remorseless about time. But when it's time to pray and work hard to achieve something spectacular, that's when our watches grow hands that tap us and tells us time is running out! It is not how long it takes you to achieve, but the quality of what you achieve. Stay focused on your goal.

029

Check this out, that someone somewhere has assigned someone invisible to take good care of you, knowing this assuredly that you're not alone; I mean this from the bottom of my heart, that we are not alone. When it seems all hope is lost, tears rolling, grounds shifting; at the end of all known roads, there and then LIGHT is come; be EXPECTANT! Don't be too careful; the hand of rescue is close by.

030

Passion and commitment are conjoined in the womb, you cannot remove passion and ignore commitment, and they come hand in hand. A life of excellence is mostly accomplished by having a consistent commitment in secret places. You achieve little with fear, but there is no limit to great success when you are passionate, committed, firm and purpose driven.

031

*O*riginality is the pathway to enduring prosperity; how rudimentary and innovative are you. Originality is the fight you give into reality. Reality is the strength you stretch toward actuality. Actuality is the reward you get for the TRUTH! We all need to live our lives on the truth; we must confess it, live it and trust it. The greatest of all men that have ever lived are the ones that lived for the truth; they trust it and their lives were the better for this. One of the most unspoken secret of becoming rich and wealthy is to discover and to know what no one has ever known or discovered.

032

*I*t's a new day, a new week and a new month; the reason all those goals are still pending is because they are not written, ideas and dreams not written; never lived beyond the owner. When you stop dreaming, stop believing, stop hoping, stop aspiring, stop ..., you are probably living in another world; not this planet!

033

*C*an an Artist paint exactly the picture of what you conceived as your future? Let the picture speak loud and clear as you exert your energy to arrive at the destination where achievers meet. Let the picture speak of your future; if the picture of your dream is speechless and dumb, it is grave and dangerous.

034

In the history of mankind, only Jesus has the testimony of the resurrection. He endured the suffering, the pains and the gruesomeness of death. He raised himself some centuries ago, raises others, still raising people today. What you do today will produce what you'll have tomorrow. Whether an instant gratification or deferred enjoyment. Victors create the future they want; while losers create the present they'll enjoy!

035

Villages are there before cities are built, your mistakes and disappointments, will always precede your results and victories. Ignore the atmosphere of impossibilities. You stand a chance to reach the touch line when you ignore the spectators. They cannot retard your effort without first gaining your attention.

036

When you believe in what you conceived, you profess it. If you can confess it, you can live what you profess; and you'll most always achieve what you've conceived. Your confession, is your profession, your profession creates your possession. Your possession will drive your decision. Your decision is what YOU are today.

037

I will rather give my all, than all being given to me; I'll rather be the best at what I do. I will always give my best! We all need to do the right so our future can be the bright. Today's pain is tomorrow's gain. There's a lesson and a life transforming message from every situation, as each page about you closes out!

038

Y ou are as big as your thoughts, and as small as your imaginations, you are as lively as your dreams and as realistic as your visions; be YOU! Never and I say never loose your hunger for greatness! People, who will achieve something great in life, never loose their hunger for that burning desire to get there. Remember cars run on petrol, airplanes run on fuel, YOU run on WHAT? You have to be burning something every day, you must then refill what has been used.

039

S ome are very selective when it comes to honoring others. It is certain we cannot please everyone; but rather honour everyone that shows up in your life. There is an angel in every man or every woman we come in contact with. I pray that when those appointed to bring us to our place of greatness appear, we'll have the discerning eyes to recognize them.

040

100 years ago we were not here; 100 years from now there is a possibility we all won't be here. Where will you be 100 months from now? During my personal thoughts; I realized once again that this planet is the only one in the universe where God created man and her activities. When you're born, you reach a certain age before knowing you are created to live in something (a soul and spirit in a body), for something or nothing. We actually no nothing before we get here (as mere children playing around); now it seems we know something (wise, now educated, with understanding); maybe nothing. It is certain that we brought nothing into this world; we'll definitely take nothing out of it, so live every day as though it's the last, love truly, give genuinely, care sincerely and help without any expectation!

041

You know what favour does? It brings you to a place you least expected. Particularly special favour is reserved for special people. It does not rain on a child of God, even if He chose to walk in the rain, the drops will shift ways, and He will walk as by dry land and blue sky. He rained favor upon me and I was drenched! What about you?

042

A life that is really worth living is the life that keeps no wrong about other people. A life that sees the bad and looks for ways to make it good. A life that takes the GOOD and carries it on; making it BETTER, a life that longs to be the best, beyond the BEST...

043

Have you heard voices before, and you looked back and saw no one? 'Someone' calls my name, I turned around, and I didn't see any one. My heart is troubled; my brain dangles within my skull. Who can help me to identify that 'someone' who calls me? Whose voice could this have been? May be my guardian angel? There's a still small voice that resides in our subconscious that guides and directs us. Don't look for it, just listen.

044

We do not exist in vacuum or created to live all by ourselves. Always call on the Lord or seek the help of someone. When you call to need the help of one person, thousands of people will be ready to help you; it is divine, honorable and rare!

045

Those who complain are fools; those who try to solve a problem are great men. That you are alive today is enough for you to be grateful to God and to do something. So what shall you do today? Just thank him and stop nagging.

046

*D*uring my search and research about God, I found out that nothing ungodly can ever be representing God, anything evil, any resemblance of deceit can only be from the devil. Reject it, detest it, flee from it, all forms of affectation; therefore beware, they all come as good and lovely people but in their hearts they are full of wickedness!

047

*Y*our attitudes and words are like a boomerang, they will always come back to you. Very few people will accept the reality to be truly sorry for their wrongdoing. The reason you don't get along with people, is the only reason they don't get in touch with you; study to get along; they would be in touch. Is your heart solid, molten or soft?

048

*T*wo things to consider before using your time for it; will it add value to other people or to you yourself. If not, I guess you discard it. Who do you sit with? How do you use your leisure? When you sit among mockers and the drunken, you will always think like them, and it is possible you'll not do anything significantly greater.

049

A re you really concerned about people? You
don't need to beg for their attention; they would
automatically devote great care to you. Love starts by
giving; does not mean you empty your bank account
for someone; it starts by considering other people, by
giving your little! Someone out there may not be able
to place a face to your gifts, but they will easily colour
in their hearts your art of kindness through gifts!

050

J esus wept; not because of the dead Lazarus, nor
the strength oozed emotions of the people crying.
He wept because of the ignorance of men! It is tragic
to see a life filled with hope, light and care suddenly
destroyed by the shackles of sin and the chains of
darkness and death. Beware of the things
that expose your life to danger!

051

S o dreamy, so different, so daring, so lovely, so
excellent, we checked where He was yesterday
but time can't wait anymore for him to see us and
say goodbye. If He had known, if He could have seen
it coming. Life and the events that comes with it,
happens unknowingly and when we least expect them.
Be your best now!

052

*L*ike a flame rises away but His works are here
   with us His voices will still be heard in the day,
at night, under the sunlight and everywhere. His
lyrics and songs are out of this world, extracted from
bottomless depth, where no other could reach except
him, so emotional, we can't even say goodbye to a soul
that sings for souls in the world; a soul that makes
much more than a difference. Words can't describe
the works that come from the bottom of his heart.
What more can we all learn from the passion
displayed by someone who gave his all
to the things he's been called upon to do.

053

*A*nyone anywhere ever reached you in any act of
   kindness? Never forget to say thank you, always
remember to share your gifts of appreciation. Reach
out and tell someone how much you mean to them and
how much their world means to you. Make yourself so
real by adding so much value to other people. You'll
mean the world to them.

054

*A*re uncommon miracles meant for the special
   ones? Can we call this luck? Or is it favor? Whose
voices are these that Bakari heard? From where
is this invincible hand that held her in the ocean?
Why is she the only survivor? To tell the story? To
accomplish an unfinished task? These and many more
questions ran through my mind when the disaster
made the headlines! I hope she understands why she
survived that plane crash; do you really understand
why you're still alive up until now?

055

When the storms of life toss you here and there, when sickness holds you down and will not let you go, do you have something you think can deliver you? Do you have someone you can trust and depend on? We all need somebody who's strong enough to withstand physical situations; we all need someone who is mighty and powerful enough to conquer spiritual and unseen circumstances; we all need someone to lean on, someone who is superhuman. Has anyone occupy this position in your life? You need not look far; God is near us all the time.

056

How would you rate your fear level on the scale 0-10 when compared with pilots, astronauts and sky divers who drive high above the earth? These are good examples of fearlessness. You have to make up your mind; don't allow fear, doubts and worry to win this battle. Confront your problems head-on. You are more than a conqueror!

057

You are what God says you are. You are what you think you are. You are not what they think you are. Don't look at the mistakes in your appearance. There are no mistakes. You will always be admired in the same way you value and cherish yourself!

058

Your life may be full of mistakes, disappointments, unrealized dreams, issues, frustrations. When it seems a particular situation has been handled, another one suddenly shows up. There is always something to fight for or against. Learn a lesson from the river that will always flow, life is all about bridges, when you cross one, there are many other bridges yet to be crossed!

059

I have never seen any man with a strong conviction to win, with the right motive and strong desire to excel and the combustive effort of hard work have any relationship with failure. Do you know anyone? Never known or seen, in anywhere and everywhere where the one termed lazy would occupy top position.

060

The Barcelona football team ascertains this fact that there are certain head(s) that the crown fits the most! So the team strives to be the first, to be the best and to stay on top. With this unshaken belief they will always get to the summit in most football competitions

061

The world mourns, his woes interject, and the Times magazine called it his talents and the tragedy. The Sun described him as the self acclaimed King of pop. He rose to stardom at the age of 6, started so well but down the line, the weirdness and the shackles of fame lay a tight hold on him. But we can forgive and forget his dash and are now relieved of the dread of his exit. Call him an Icon, call him a legend, and I call him the musical giant of the 21st century. His name inscribed on a platter of gold, written among stars and the spirits. Eventually he fell from grace! What an inspiration for all of us. Americans went to bed and cannot contain the grief of his death. About 6.5 billion people woke up to realize that the cancerous demon of death eventually ate up this special boy, Michael Jackson, popularly called Jaco... at the end of your life time, when the curtain will be drawn on you, will you be remembered for anything? And if par chance you are remembered, what will the world remember you for?

062

Little wonder the Angel said, go into the temple and tell them all the words of this life! Words written in text books actually help medical Doctors operate those living and semi-living humans; words written in books make Pilots fly those gigantic planes; words written in the scriptures, raises the dead, heals the sick... Wouldn't you rather read your BIBLE; hear-in lies wealth of words for every facets of life!

063

One of the most unforgettable moments in life, is when the bad suddenly becomes good, when you witness the change you strongly desired. When all is said and done, may you find help where others struggle for help! Although this would only come when there is a strong desire.

064

Don't have this mindset that all is over when you're faced with a compelling situation that makes your heart pants and headaches. Know this for sure that you're created such that when new things show up in your life, you'll always have the aptitude and the proneness to withstand anything as such!

065

The difference between drinking and eating is that one is faster than the other, the difference between you and the other person is TIME. There is a place where everyone is called to stay; can you discover your own place and time? In no time, may this be said about you, that all your dreams came true!

066

Maybe all you needed to do was simply to ask, but your ego would not allow you do so. You may have to put away your status; you may have to undress yourself from your pride and then walk up to someone and tell it all. All you needed to be satisfied in life may have been handed over to someone close to you, and this someone is busy waiting for you to come claim what belongs to you.

067

Questions keep coming, doubts flooding the hearts of men, words as stones rolling down the internet...Has technology reached its peak? Yesterday an old technology was the delight of so many people. Today, a new technology springs a big surprise. Tomorrow, yet another technology will leave questions in our hearts. Opportunities are limitless.

068

Someone once said that planes will fly in the sky, and today we all travel by air. I also believe that one day humans will not just visit the moon; they'd visit other solar systems and even live in other planets. When you predict it, believe it, it would happen someday.

069

*P*atience sometime could be frustrating; when
you're desperate for result. Be rest assured your
patience is part of God's original plan. May God help
us to prioritize things that are important and give
less attention to junks.

070

I wonder why people willingly disobey basic
principles though they know the consequence. You
will always be re warded for what you did and also
what you fail to do. There is always a price for every
prize; paid and unpaid. When the beginning and the
underlying basis of life is destroyed what shall the
ignorant do?

071

D iscovered there is so much to read like me? So
much to learn that I don't even know where to
start. You know what I did; I just start anyway. You'll
belong in the best READERSHIP when you cultivate
the simple habit of just reading something every day.
Reading to me is like eating! If you've not gotten to
the point where reading satisfies your hunger for
food; I guess you are not ready to face the many
battles ahead. The simple thing that really matters in
life doesn't always appear simple!

072

A re you aware that the road to success is always
under construction, and that everyone is the
engineer of his or her road that leads to success,
so keep working, keep constructing, building and
rebuilding your road to success.

073

D o you have anyone in heaven? He that sits up
there is very ready to be your strength, your
shield, your portion, your deliverer, your shelter, your
strong tower, and your very present help in times of
need!

074

Some said arguably that our prayers are never answered. They quickly forgotten the gifts of life, the priceless words we speak; the ability to see... Your very thoughts have the power to become real. Filter them if you will find comfort seeing them come through!

075

The farther you've gone in the journey you set out for yourself; the nearer you are to end of the road, keep moving. Distractions are there to tell you that many unseen forces are contending for your destiny; you know what to do? Just IGNORE them or use the strongest weapon anybody can use on this planet which is FAITH!

076

If falling or failing is a major problem, I guess the whole world would be neglected by now; the good news is when you fall, you rise again. Keep trusting, believing, hoping, expecting, seeing, trying, and doing; these actions combined create the greats and keep recreating them! Your reward ceremony is closer than you realize; it is the beginning of the middle of a half end year!

077

The high way, can never be the only way; there is an alternative; it's very easy to find the low way, to walk the high way, you need FAITH! Easy to find the low way; very easy to walk the low; but for the excited, courageous and highly motivated fellow, the high way, all the way!

078

You cannot be critical to the world, if you are not being criticized; if it doesn't work out today, it would work out someday; so keep working and making it work. Faultfinders are there to make you a gold-digger. They are there to make you discover the gold in YOU!

079

Do you think every new Monday isn't different from previous ones? It all depends on you; you can make and create the difference you wish to see in everyday. Make your every new day grand. Make it a new brand!

080

Is there any peace on earth comparable with the serenity and equanimity you experienced when you first got saved and baptized? Make up your mind, be firm, resolute and unyielding about this; don't turn around to the things you've left behind!

081

*D*on't be discouraged and don't give up when men fail to promote you, but believe that the future belongs to those who stand in the realities of their dreams, just take your soul by the hand and let your spirit fly!!!

082

*C*ars refill at petrol stations, Horses refill at the river banks, Eagles refill on mountain tops; where do you refill, realign and renew? The force of persistence cannot be suppressed; never give up until you get what you want!

083

*T*he best time to hold on and persist is when you reach the place where the discouraged give up, where the unbeliever says it's impossible, where cowards bow out. This is the place where you stand up; never to give up!

084

*H*e told the sun to shine for the day, He told the oceans not to move past a point, He can command the situation of your life to hold on. Trust Him, He is Greater than all! As I stood by the coast of the Atlantic few days ago; I gazed, sighed and marveled at the words that held those waters in their line.

085

Web 1.0 is the popular www, websites, Google, (they are non interactive). Web 2.0 is the widely accessed Facebook, twitter, blogs, Wikipedia (they are all interactive). What should the world expect in web 3.0.? web 1.0 is almost fading away; the world is crazy and excited about web 2.0. What should we expect in web 3.0? The word is not stagnant; keep moving.

086

I sometimes wonder why the world is saturated with inequality. Some are presidents, while some are paupers. Some have more than enough, while some others can't even afford anything. Some are high flyers, while some are low. I really don't know why but, I recognize that we are living in the same world and there is enough space even on earth that everyone can afford to secure a spot.

087

Look beyond the storm. Walk the other side; all would soon be calm, and the wave would be over past. It would soon be over! Cherish the freedom you have; you cannot afford to lose it!

088

Shower so much love on the people you know and the people that are dear to you. Make them feel loved; find time to create the excitement they will never forget when you're not there. Truth is they will not always be there.

089

Don't ever feel you are alone when trouble comes; you have a father in heaven. Bear this in mind before you were born he had promised he will never leave or forsake you. It takes just a phone call - an effectual fervent prayer.

090

We must admit our ignorance before the maker of a product. We see the beginning, but God our maker, the ultimate manufacturer knows what the future holds. He knows all things. He will handle every circumstance for our good if we allow him to take charge!

091

Be a LASER (Leadership Attained Strategically with Excellence and Results) every day, every way and anywhere, because you've got the light that can cut through any, and I mean every issues and circumstances of life. Never let the light go off!

092

Knowledge is everything; I mean everything in the very things. Everything you want to know has been written down by someone. Seek nothing else first, but knowledge.

093

A man without strong belief and hope is like a knife without an edge, how will he cut through the difficulties of life, how will he cope with the raging storms of this world?!?!?

094

Go to the gym, play football, play basket ball, play tennis, at least for your own good, partake in at least one sport; this will help you to keep fit. It can add more years to your life.

095

Quietness could be a symbol of strength and submission. If you know you will not be able to say anything good when you're angry, its better you keep quite. This is an ultimate test for self-control!

096

Information is the key that unlocks gigantic doors to an unparallel breakthrough, how often do you care to know? How will you give what you don't have? Knowledge comes by knowing what you don't know. Read for you life!

097

"I love you", "I forgive you", "I am sorry". These are complete sentences; you don't need to say any words after these. They will leave a lasting and enduring impression about you.

098

The journey to the top could be easier when compared with the rigors of staying and sustaining top positions. The greatest secret to the tallest of all success stories is the inner strength that stays positive, the insatiable desire to keep moving. No matter how tough the realities in your life always saturate your environment with the positive.

099

We can copy God in this... He is always busy; busy creating men, sending them as babies into the world; are you busy or lazy? If only you'll start! It's just one step... one step at a time; you'll get to the top!

100

Problems are there as a confirmation that solutions will always be available, problems are there for you to know that solutions are also standing so close. Always look for ways to resolve an issue, rather than nagging, complaining, name calling, angry, frustrated...May your life be meaningful enough to bring meaning to others. May you be a channel of blessings and a cloud of hope to your generation.

101

Reason is not automatic; those that deny it will not be condemned by it, and will not be questioned by it; but those that allow it will end up adding or removing something from what they had.

102

In passing through here, you need to realize that time counts, and people live life almost in the same way some had lived in the past, making little or no impact in life. What is the quality of the life you are living? You simply want to pass by or you want to make an impact.

103

There comes a time in every man's life, when you've got to make up your mind what you'll live for. That's why every day, every hour, every minute and every second I remind myself thus: "the life that I live is not my own; for me to live is gain!"

104

I have often heard that people have the fear of failure, but I think what they really suffer is the fear of success. If you fear to fail, you fear to succeed.

105

If He could hold down great oceans - the Atlantic, the Pacific - and commanded them not to move; He can hold down the activities of your enemies!

106

There is something to accomplish in your personal life; there are assignments to complete in your public life; there are bridges to cross in your emotional life; but a truly successful man is the one who shows the result of what he has done. Always strive to give your best and the fruit of your labor will speak for itself.

107

Mother's day celebrated all over the world, does she understand how much you truly love her? Not just in words, but in kindness and deed. If yes, take a deep breath... Always honor your mother; length of days this singular act will add to your life.

108

When you give your time to ensuring everything concerning others is well and alright, you should not be surprised about this; they will give their life in return!

109

You will never go wrong, never, and I say never, if you act and work the way your boss chose, even if it's not convenient. Strive to submit yourself to established authority.

110

Envy is a Sign that the light in you is getting dim, dimmer and darkening, lighten your life with faith and love in other people. It is never too late to speak a word of life into someone's life; be it in the morning, at noon or at night!

111

Follow your dreams and even dance with it. The possibility that you may fail in your struggle should not deter you from the fight for a cause you always believe to be true!

112

Don't stop giving! Let's start giving - give in the day, give at noon, give at night, and give everything to anyone who needs your gift. You cannot lack any good thing when you cultivate the habit of giving.

113

*B*e yourself no matter how hard you try to please someone, there is another out there you displease. Be real to yourself; the world worships the original!

114

*T*here is something in a chicken that restricts her from flying; the dove goes into hiding when the storm hits; an eagle knows the sign of a storm long before it breaks. You are created to soar like an eagle – not to live like a chicken!

115

*T*here is nothing done in the secret, that will not be in the open, there is nothing hidden that will not be exposed; there is nothing more secure, most realistic and ever peaceful than living for the TRUTH, than living for others, than being a light in this thick and very dark; I mean terribly dark world! I now understand for sure when the savior said ' 'ye are the light of the world!

116

*Y*ou have made thousands of decisions – most of them were 'cold' decisions but some of them were 'hot', the consequences of making a poor choice could be devastating. What could possibly go wrong if you had pounded yam instead of toast for breakfast?

117

*L*ife is full of competition. You'll always have a competitive edge when you have the ability to see far into the future, rather than struggle on without vision and specific direction.

118

*Y*ou will lay up gold as dust and silver as sand, - all you'll need to do is to keep dreaming and keep believing. Saturate your mind with faith and trust; these two go hand in hand

119

*W*hatever has a beginning must definitely have an ending. You will not regret your actions when you endure to receive the result of something you started. Time may appear too slow on your side, be patient, because there will always be a bright morning after waiting long through the night.

120

*D*reams get you out of your bed in the morning, put a smile on your face and a bounce in your step; cherish your dreams; they are taking you somewhere.

121

*L*ife is a stretch of battles – you fight wars within and without. Killing, hatred and wickedness exist in low and high places. All of these speak of ignorance, naivety and how myopic the human mind could be; it is darkened, disillusioned and deluded. Activating ignorance, supporting wickedness and confessing hatred to fellow humans will grow if you do not find time to enhance your knowledge, what you know is what you fight for; it is what you think you are; it's what you compete with; it's what you guide jealously! What you don't know are the things you cannot see; the things that are spiritual; the things that are even physical but not visible enough for the human eyes to behold! These are the things that matters, because the things that are seen are actually temporal, ephemeral, and outgoing!

122

*D*on't ever forget your source and the people that helped you to the top. They can keep you up there, and yet they can pull you down and back to where they first met you, be wise!

123

*T*reasure a friend who generates energy and enthusiasm towards your dreams and goals! True friends are always around to make sure all your desires come through.

124

S ometimes our greatest challenge is to get inside our own heads to understand what makes us click. You have the singular assignment to know why you feel and behave the way you do.

125

D esired something greatly? To reach it, run with it, if running is fast, walk, if walking is difficult, try crawling; be sure you're moving. When discouragement stands at the door, you're sure encouragement is knocking and waiting; which one would you indulge? With passion and strong belief anything is possible!

126

T he hardest reflection of many lives is remembering what they could have done right or done better. Do give everyday your best. Take charge! As simple as they are; instructions are required for construction while some instructions could lead to destruction. Never complain about what you permit!

127

A s long as you can spend at least 30minutes everyday on the things you plan to achieve this year; you will achieve.

128

Your destiny is in your hands! Oh lest I forget, I was asked to inform you that your destiny is no longer in God's hands... You are the only one that would determine everything about you. You are the captain. Sail your ship!!

129

The disappointments of today are the convincing signposts that your miracles are right ahead. A golden opportunity - a favorable circumstance for progress and advancement - could disguise in grilling difficulties!

130

Can a bird fall in love with a fish? If they do where will they live? So you cannot fall in love with a creature outside your realm of existence.

131

Parents would be accountable for all the children they brought into this world. Eli was an example; he unknowingly permitted treachery. Children who are rude, unruly and riotous are ignorantly reducing the lifespan of their parents; you better live right for their sake.

132

When nothing else would do; ... Love will lift you up! It could lift someone out there who is scattered, battered, tattered and shattered by the fears of our world. It's a potent force; never be short of LOVE.

133

True love speaks in tender tone and listens with a caring heart. True love covers all your mistakes, even though we all know how imperfect we are. Do you think someone loves you truly?

134

Don't be deceived by their showers of praise, if you really want to know the truth about your actions, ask those who had done it before! Dissatisfaction is a seed you'll sow to get satisfaction; satisfied with where you are? If yes, I guess you're in life's farm doing nothing!

135

Friendship is all about giving, no matter how small; give and you shall receive the same measure. How often do you love people, yet you never give them something worth a penny?

136

The whole essence of life starts by helping someone. To get to the top, you'll need to serve other people. Service, I mean excellent service; can lift you to the pinnacle of excellence - the summit.

137

You fall for everything, you permit and allow anything. No orders, less standards and more activities. A man without a resounding reason for living is like a broom in use by everyone; how will he cope with the rubbish of this life!

138

Doing what you enjoy, lasts, it endures, longer than expected, decade upon decades it remains, you don't force it; it flows and comes natural. Over the years you suddenly are now words that your ears allowed, events that picked your eyes, and the thoughts that intercept your mind.

139

When Monday morning comes, know that Friday night is a few seconds away; what you have to do on Monday, don't let up for Friday, because procrastination kills! Procrastination is a thief of life; procrastination draws people closer to their grave!

140

Your decisions today will affect all of your unborn generations, be careful and seek God, before making all your decisions. The quality of your life most especially depends on the quality of your thoughts, what sits on the throne of your heart.

141

Without faith and strong belief you cannot achieve even beyond your reach. I think it is even impossible to be alive without an iota of faith!

142

Dare to be different! What an immense power you'll have over your life when you posses distinct aim! Regardless of what people say, or how you feel, be different to make a difference!

143

When you stand for something, you will attract the attention of the world, people will want to find out what you particularly stand for. Alas! You will be excited the number of followers you'll have when you passionately follow through what you're living for. All great men with great followers stood for something.

144

You *may not have all the time in the world to keep strategizing. You may not have all of lifetime to decide on your career path. You need to make up your mind what pathway you want to tread in life. Decide today how you'll spend your years, and every other thing will fall in place.*

145

Strangers are the strangest secrets to unlocking supernatural doors; these doors could be positive or otherwise. Learn to treat strangers with caution and courtesy; you never know who is seeing what you cannot see.

146

If your imaginations are filled with positive thoughts, they could come alive, because our imaginations can take us anywhere, I mean anywhere in the universe! Moreover, if your imagination are filled with impossibilities, they'll happen so quickly!

147

True love batters all fears; genuine love scatters every prejudice; and an unconditional love from you can rejuvenate life in a dying soul!

148

Looking for something new, something different, you may need to search deeply than mere scratching the surface. You want to be wise, fear God!

149

Malicious software such as viruses, spywares and trojans are dangerous and can render a computer useless in split seconds. So also are malicious people - they are infected with pathogenic viruses and can sniff life out of others.

150

Happy people don't judge themselves by what others do or have; they don't measure their success by the standards of others. Only failures and unhappy people judge themselves by the standards of others.

151

People that are truly happy, forgive other people from the very bottom of their hearts. You only have the freedom to create what will make you happy.

152

Some people witness history in the making, some people are part of historical events being made, while some people make history happen; what part of history are you fulfilling? Are you on this planet as a spectator or an artiste; are you here to be watched or to watch?

153

*H*ero Pilot Chesley Sullenberger (who guided a
jet safely on the surface of Hudson River in the
United States) was to attend Obama inauguration;
with courage and diligence, you'll stand before kings!

154

*G*od hanged the earth upon nothing! He compassed
great oceans of the world – the Atlantic, the
Pacific... with invisible bounds! He has the
lifetime for your greatness!

155

*It is very impossible for a normal human being
to be in more than one place at the same time, so
why do you worry about what will happen, or what
has happened over there, and how this or that will
happen to you, tomorrow, or then. Just make sure
you're doing something that is good enough to affect
people even though you are not there.*

156

*Seal up your mind against every negative thoughts,
set your thoughts on things that are beautiful.
Men who have confronted the greatest of dangers and
difficult occasions always bath their hearts in
good thoughts.*

157

*Sometimes all you need to recover from breaking
down is rest! Working too much or being too
engaged in different activities brings great dangers
to your health. So learn to go back and rest. Maybe
that's all you need to redeem your image, from all the
mistakes tiredness have caused you.*

158

*The best and cheapest way to really reward people
who have done kind deeds to you is to say thank
you, in a big way!*

159

*L*earn not to look at faults and mistakes that are in other people; always appreciate what other people will have to contribute, no matter how little!

160

*T*ake time to listen attentively; take time to jot down important points; take time to be patient; you will remember everything and do much more than expected when you give full attention to instructions and accord maximum concentration to details.

161

*L*earn to hold back; learn to bridle your tongue, because when you make a wrong statement it will be attributed to you. You need to weigh the consequences of what you say because what comes out of your mouth are the things you'll be judged by, not your thoughts.

162

*G*od loves praise, how much more human beings. Praise your boss, your friends and yourself; it goes a long way to improve their performance!

163

*H*ow prepared were you in the morning of the month of January? As the mornings close out, the night comes when no one is working, and before you realize it, we are already in the middle of the year, while December is knocking at the door.

164

L ooking within, and looking without, looking
inward, and looking outwards; you're an
embodiment of wonders and miracles!

165

A recurring motif of being remembered. Year in
year out, decades in decades out, century in
century out, millennium in millennium out, people
come in and people go out, people are remembered
and so many more are forgotten, billion and
quadrillions of humans have walked this earth, only
a few are remembered, will you be remembered for
something?

166

S earching through the history of men that have
been crowned as best in one field or the other, I
resolved in my heart that you should never think
about ignoring or putting aside... the days of little
beginnings!

167

N ever lose hope of your horizon; never sell it to
impending circumstances. If the truth be told,
the difference between winners and losers, success
and failure, problems and solutions is the attitude of
whoever is involved!

168

When I meditate on how man's heart beats non-stop 72 times in 60 seconds, I commend and appreciate the great God who created this system called man. Always there to ensure the beating never stops, always there even when we are asleep, always watching over his creatures, what a wonderful father; are you a good father to your children?

169

Please keep your God-given endowment up, you are a leader. You are a shining Star; an illuminating Light. Therefore as a building that is set on a hill, you cannot be hidden.

170

*F*aith is calling and relating the future tense in past tense. It is the assurance that the future is already in the past!

171

*T*he life that really matters and worth living here, and living forever, is a selfless life, a life spent and lived for others. Let your life be worth living?

172

A man who is calm at provocation from his superiors and his subordinates develops the third eye. He sees farther than the impatient one; he knows better, and stays away when danger looms.

173

*D*on't stop working, don't stop trying, don't stop trusting, don't stop all the good little things, they will help you get there. Can you boldly say this to yourself, "I've gone too far to consider quitting".

174

*Y*ou are fearfully and wonderfully made, thanks for being much more than the world could ever imagine to someone, you will get there. Are you aware that someone knows your end before you were even born, that someone is ready to take you through

175

It is easier to always speak the truth than telling lies. Can you see the difference, one is speaking and the other is telling, one is powerful and the other one is weak. There is no controversy, what you do in secret, but you you're afraid to expose would likely create torment and unrest in you...Repent!

176

In passing through here, one needs to realize that time counts and the same life, the same people, made of the same components live life almost in the same way some lived in the past, and some the immediate. While it may appear divine for some to live in the future, it is natural for people to live in the present. What part of time are you living in?

177

When you are on the right side, when you are on God's side, be rest assured; no evil shall befall you; neither shall any plague come near your dwelling place, if you can only believe!

178

It's never too late to start preparing; never too early to think of starting! It will only be late when your qualification as either (Mr. or Mrs.) is being replaced by LATE!

179

*M*ake sure you're always with a person who knows what it takes to be on top. When you say there is casting down, you need someone to assure you that there is lifting up even when you're down! Get the right companion.

180

*H*appy people don't judge themselves by what others do or have; they don't measure themselves with the yardstick of others. Be HAPPY! Focus on what gives you joy and fulfillment.

181

*E*veryone needs progress, everyone wants to be promoted, but the last time I checked my compass of life I was directed convincingly that promotion comes neither from the east nor from the west; it comes from God! Go to God for yours; He will give to whoever cares to ask!

182

*N*o matter how little your act of kindness, the little assistance you gave, the unexceptional help you rendered, the alms you dropped in an outstretched arm - will never go unremembered; it will remain indelible in the hearts of men!

183

If you try your best and it's not working, I guess the quality of your best is not so good as to outsmart your better. Don't give in!

184

Stop rushing out every morning as if something is chasing you. Always ask yourself this question: "when I left my room this morning, did I saturate and bathe the day in prayer?"

185

There is no situation or circumstances that will show up in your life without an alternative route for escape. You decide to face the situation with an immediate decision within split seconds or you delay your decision. No matter how hard or how simple, a quick and decisive decision from a determined and a no-nothing-person will always yield an expected outcome.

186

People tend to be more careful, sober, remorseful and tender hearted when they find themselves in life endangering situations. Truth is, when all is well, when it seems you are in control that is when you should raise the bar of your sobriety.

187

A man without passionate faith is like a ship without a captain, how will he sail past the wind and the turbulent issues of life?

188

If you tune up your ear, open wide your eyes and free your heart, you will hear things that have never been heard, see things that are invisible to others and understand revelations beyond normal human comprehension.

189

Some battles are fought on horses, some are fought with most recent technologies and some are fought with strong armies, but those who fight on their knees, have got victory in all the battles of life.

190

You may need to stay awake if you really want to achieve more than every other person that sleep all through the nights!

191

Laughter is the cheapest drug on earth that can rejuvenate life in a dying soul. To stay healthy - be happy; don't keep grudges. Laugh

192

*A*re you aware that the solution to leaving your sick bed on time is to remind yourself everyday that, "this is not where I belong". You have to recite this to yourself.

193

*L*oneliness is not lack of people, at times you need to be alone, and this is when you can prepare yourself, equipped and strong enough to face the crowd. Lonely periods are seasons when leaders are being molded and fortified for the challenges ahead!

194

*T*hose who drive and travel at night are prone to less danger than those who drive and travel during the day; night travelers are more careful than daylight travelers. It affirms that driving is all about taking care and being cautious!

195

*A*re you aware that the road to success isn't just a road? Roads to success are many, but whoever endures to the end, will attain success.

196

*Y*ou will not always have the strength to do all you're doing today. Work hard enough now for you will not have the strength like when you first arrived here on earth!

197

Fearful people are weak and inconsistent, and may not achieve any major thing. Show me a man that stands for the truth, a man that's worth its salt, a man that ensure fairness and discharge his duties without prejudice and self seeking interests; I will show you a bold man, strong enough to deliver results in the face of wickedness and evil pretenders.

198

Don't even try to reward evil for good. No matter how you present good as incomplete or undeserving, it will ever remain superior to wickedness. Never compare them; they are parallel lines, they will never meet – evil and good!

199

A lot of people are confused, and this confusion is magnified in this simple delusion that lies, a lying tongue and a deceptive life bring quick reward, and are convenient ways of life. I dare say that truth will always stand tall even though all other buildings have been shaken and rumbled by the quake of time. Truth endures! Speaking and living the truth is the best and the most convenient way of life. It will give you hope for the future, your generation will reap re-rewards from the truth legacy you will leave behind.

200

*D*on't be discouraged and don't give up when men fail to promote you, but believe this that the future belongs to those who wait in the reality of their dreams. Just take your soul by the hand and let your spirit fly!!!

201

*T*here are always two sides to life - the positive and the negative. Which side of life are you? Let your thoughts and actions; your dreams and aspirations merge inexorably with the positive.

202

*J*ust came back from a retreat tagged, "stretching your potentials", learnt that we can create a smarter world, in this ever changing world by consistently stretching ourselves, by going the extra mile, by thinking differently, by just putting more effort.

203

*Y*ou are not alone in this world; there are other over 6 billion people out there. Guess what? They are waiting for you, for you to shine! Maybe their success would be kindled by your story. Your testimony could be all that they need to reach their own destiny!

204

The difference between natural and supernatural is that extreme quality 'super'; how often do you ensure superior standards in your output? Do not celebrate mediocrity. Stand out!

205

With haughtiness, pride and arrogance you'll find it difficult to get to the top in a sane and respectable society where everyone loves to be among; but with humility, quietness and poise, honour will chase you and possibly overtake you.

206

Do you know what it means to dance in the rain, if you really know, how often then do you? Is it when life is worth living... or when it seems all hope is lost? Again I ask; how often do you dance in the rainy and torrential occurrences of life?

207

Have you learnt how to stay happy and excited though all seems not to be well? Don't go around carrying bold face and moody countenance when you are faced with life issues. Remember no matter how hot the sun hits during the day, when the night draws near the sun hides its face, and the cold night breeze takes over. Every single thing has a specific timeline.

208

A re you a wind without mouth but produces indistinct sound and voices? Are you a brook or a tree with continuous sound, but no one to answer? Why do you murmur and complain with discontent and dissatisfaction? Be in charge; stop grumbling. Take control, be responsible for everything; I mean anything that shows up in your life. You can handle it; believe it or not!

209

A lways learn to ensure you protect the interest of other people. Give yourself to others, not always seeking your own, and if possible never retaining all for yourself. I can assure you people abound who will fight and protect all that belong to you, when you ensure the oppressed is settled.

210

D eception, lie and hypocrisy are everywhere; this is a loophole. An uncommon way of life is to stand, and to stand firm for the truth, and you will win and save many!

211

T he difference between BITTER and BETTER is the I and E. Both alphabets determine what happens next in our lives, in our universe. It only takes one singular thing to happen around you and all of your good will become better!

212

A lways allow them to push all the work to you. Unknowingly they are building you for something bigger, bolder and better. Work as if you don't need the money; make yourself so valuable that you'll become invaluable!

213

Y ou don't need all the information in the world to know your next move. All you needed is the power of intuition, the ability to make quick and sound decisions based on minimum information!

214

W hy do you complain so much about what people are suppose to do for you. Why do you think people owe you so much? If a price tag is placed on walking; how much would we owe God? Friends rather than thinking of what people owe you think about what you can give; you have nothing to lose when you deeply care for other people.

215

M uch more than imagination, much more than mental creation, much more than being inventive, now easier than getting started. You must and can believe your entire mental picture; all things are possible to him or her that believes!

216

The journey to the top could be easier when compared with the rigors of staying and sustaining top positions. All you have to do to remain standing and to remain on top is to rise each time you fall!

217

There are so many planets in the universe, but the earth was chosen for human habitation. Whoever created life on this beautiful planet must have believed in its potentials above every other planets, and must have chosen man above every other forms and other existence for his exceeding capacities. Therefore, whoever created you to exist with this generation must have believed in you, must have had a purpose for you, must have seen that you will not leave this place without making an impact... for as I woke up this morning, and gazed through my balcony, I knew that night comes, suddenly, when no man can actually work. I must make a difference! Say this to yourself every day.

218

We worry a lot about what we think we don't have and forget the things we freely really had, while others have more. There is nothing more rewarding than a heart of gratitude. There is no painting more colourful than the art of appreciation.

219

Do you think your life would be perfect if..., you had a better pay job, a better house, a better bank account, an expensive car, a better spouse, a better boss...? It is your choice to decide what makes life better for you. What is the most important to you may be least important to someone else.

220

The difference between the wise and the foolish is that fools would most naturally act based on their personal opinion, without analysis, and without considering other person's ideas.

221

Am looking forward to a day when morning will cease to be, and night will be a rhythm of the past. Do you think there is anything new under the heaven?

222

Did you ever recite the national pledge? "You pledged to your country, to be faithful, loyal and honest, to serve her with all your strength…" And you loot the treasury, kill, steal public funds, mismanage public offices, and you think your deeds will not hunt you? The lyrics are spirits, and without an iota of doubt, if you've recited those words and you still go ahead, hurting your country, am afraid…, the consequences are cataclysmic.

223

A true champion is someone who believes in greatness. Greatness means understanding the secret of joy by washing the feet of others. It means; becoming like a little child, and giving the whole of you to serve others.

224

*I*s it true that early to bed and early to rise makes a man healthy, wealthy and wise? Today we pursue riches and success in the environment so vigorously that for some it is: late to bed and early to rise makes a man unhealthy, poor and foolish!

225

*T*he new is conceived in the old to be revealed and the old is released in the new to be reviewed! Don't throw away your old, and always cherish the new that shows up in your life!

226

*N*o matter what public opinion and suggestion is about you, they will only matter and have strong credence when your opinion about yourself takes the same route as their assertions.

227

*W*ill keep writing until the ink reservoir of the world get exhausted; and then keep praising God until the whole world knows that He lives. Never, and I say never stop doing the things that will bring out the best in you! Don't stop being the best!

228

Those who are quick in attributing the fault of failure blame the situation on their friends, colleagues, neighbours, parents, and even our country; they could easily be drowned in the murky waters of depression and heart disease. Those who, however, hold themselves responsible for whatever shows up in their lives overcome the vicissitudes of life and are blessed with a healthy heart.

229

I think you will be wasting your time and effort asking him to go the extra mile. Are you satisfied watching him go the normal mile? For a lazy man going the extra mile is not an option, he murmurs and lackadaisically approaches the normal and everybody's mile!

230

The fear of today is the reality of yesterday, and it is the hope of tomorrow. Take the bull of your fear by the horn, and let courage and strength lead you!

231

*H*ave you ever found yourself in a situation where the stage is set for you to tell us where you belong? Have you ever asked yourself these questions: "who am I? What stuff am I made of? What are my values? Where do I belong? The you can never give what you don't have; neither do you speak farther than the capacity of your memory. From the abundance of the heart the mouth speaks truly. Always check your memory bank and ensure it is constantly fed with the right words.

232

*W*e all have something inside of us that is created by the creator and is specifically unique to us; we all can start by giving that thing to our world. It could be our time, our values, our presence and a whole lot of many other things. You will never be left alone when you've sold yourself into giving all into the lives of so many people.

233

*W*hen men praise you so much for your exceeding success and achievement and forget to honour your creator, they are pushing you gradually away from the source of your strength. Don't be carried away by their approval, rather lay all your trophies down and give glory to your God and your creator.

234

You know sometime we feel frustrated, disappointed and impatient about the things our living really hangs on; about the things that brings satisfaction and fulfillment. We prayed, worked, asked and waited to get this particular thing that will bring out the wow word from our mouth. How long should we wait when it seems time is counting down on us?

235

The old saying goes that hope deferred will make the soul weary. Always remember though that hope deferred is not hope deterred; it's not hope annulled. Hope deferred is hope confirmed, for why should we hope for what we already have and can see? Keep waiting; keep believing; for someday your waiting would soon be over!

236

Time is always there as a reminder that we are getting closer to something - to the very mark of the expected glory.

237

It's hard to tell how fast the clock ticks when we dream about the future... when you wish to be married, have children, afford all that you want... you always feel there is still time. The future may be in a land far, far away, but the future you really desire is just like the tomorrow you long to see; it gets closer as the night walks away!

238

You should define it today, don't wait till tomorrow. You should write them down now, do not procrastinate. Whatever it is that will give you satisfaction and ultimate fulfillment when you say good bye to this world should be accomplished. You shouldn't give sleep to your eyelids until you see all of those things come to pass.

239

In a few months time you'll say goodbye to this year, have you achieved all you set out to accomplish this year? If your answer is yes, a big congratulation to you! If yours is no, it's never too late, to start all over again! For you, the year just began!

240

Wisdom was there when the foundation of this world was formed. Wisdom knows everything about anything. The difference between the rich and the poor is the level of wisdom available to each. To be wise, then and then, we need to invest in our thoughts, invest in thinking; we need to open our minds to the things that will make us as wise as Solomon.

241

Ever been loved by anyone? Some have never seen love, so tearful. If you have ever known love; all is incomparable to God's eternal love. Before the end of the year, we would celebrate your reward ceremony provided you've faithfully rewarded someone else!

242

You don't need to be there to know what's going on over there. All you needed is to have someone that's always there; someone who is everywhere at every hour and in every situation. Someone whose voice will be there when all other voices thin out!

243

The difference between us all - the rich and the poor, the great and the small, the wise and the foolish, the known and the unknown, the creator and the created, the selector and the selected, the fortunate and the unfortunate - is not in the clothes we wear or the way we look. The difference is the way we THINK! Invest judiciously in your thinking methodology, now and today, and while you can!

244

Don't be weary in doing what is right. Keep doing well, and keep on doing what you know and think is right. There will always be a season for reward.

245

We often quickly forgot the trophies, the medals, the certificates that have sprung smiles on our faces. Our successes may be little, but we've all had moments in our lives when we set out to achieve some particular things and we made it to the end. Every little success is an outstanding success. It attracted some loud voices from the inside that screamed: "yes, I made it!" Learn to remember and cherish such moments in your life; they will always be a balm when rusty obstacles show up.

246

You know you have done so many things to achieve that feat - the sacrifices you made, the sleepless nights you endured, the fasting you stretched, the standing you insure, the waiting that lasted, the diligence you displayed, and so many other efforts you invested - all of which revealed the best in you. They turned your nights into day and your sorrows into rivers of joy. They are the things you will continue to do; they'll drive you through the rough road to the smooth top on the mountain. They'll help you stay on top, but if you ignore them... your expectations may be stunted!

247

We all have waiting times in our lives. Mothers have to wait for nine months to sail through the unknown to bring forth the known. Creatures have to wait through the nights to resume a bright and at times sudden and new morning. The earth have to rotates 365 days, waiting, wailing, and moving round the sun to complete a cycle and then call in the new year. Nationals have to be patient for some years to elect a new president. Warriors have to wait during the seasons' fierce wars to secure a victory in the battle field. You will also have to wait for some time to be able to announce your own victory. In your waiting times, remain steadfast and unrepentantly hopeful!

248

*H*e never promised a turbulent free flight; He never said the storms won't rage, so why are you afraid? Why do you scare the hell out of yourself and the people around you, especially when your feet is about to board that flight, or when the aircraft drifts and swifts? Whenever I heard his still small assuring voice, I hold on to the promise that we'll touch down safely. He knows the end from the beginning! His words give me Goose bumps, what about you?

249

*I*n my hour of meditation, so many questions run through my spirit mind, I then thought it good to share this with you, though we all unconsciously live by something, for something and in some things. Have you found where you belong? If you ignorantly dance to any tune, any song and any rhythm, plugged or unplugged, you will be living for anything. What a season to reassign and renew what takes priority in your life. Where do you belong? What do you stand for? And then who are you?

250

*I*n your darkest hour when all things are just nothing but packed, when you feel so lonely and it seems no one is even around to say I care, maybe you'll need that hour to speak to someone greater and even older than time. There is always someone, standing there in the corner of the room in your heart, saying, talk to me; I will handle all your worries and cares. My friend, it's time to pray!

251

*A*ppreciate the people around you, especially
those people that are there to make success out
of you. I discovered that people around us, - some we
ignore and give less value and attention – are the
ones that really do love us. They can do anything for
us whether we merit them or not. Your mother, your
father, your siblings, your friends, your sweet heart,
your colleagues – they are the people that really
matter; they'll always believe in you!

252

*W*e must keep our best attitude in constant
repair. We must wear it like a garment, clean
it when dirt stains it, dry clean it when it is wet – the
attitude of doing things in a better way, not following
the status quo; an attitude of altitude, an attitude
that never dies must ultimately be sustained. I will
try once again; I will try to make it better. I will do
it with a new concept, breaking patterns and then
making the whole wide world a better place!

253

*G*reat satisfaction comes when you encourage,
appreciate and admire the things you freely
really had; and you complain less about the things
you really quickly desired!

254

Guard your heart with all that you have, with all your strength, with all your might; for the enemy's target points directly to your heart. The heart is at the centre of everything. Once it's afflicted with worry, doubt, fear, discouragement, even the greatest men in history fall down, fall apart, and fall prey to the insignificant weaponry in the arsenal of the evil one!

255

When we cross a bridge in our lives, we're excited about our achievement and we talk about it with glitz and satisfaction. But as we jubilate about our breakthrough, we must forget the things that are before. There are so, so many mountains to climb, so many bridges to cross. Our focus should always be on the next strategy!

256

Hymns are words composed as songs, they are extraordinary and trans-generational; beyond ordinary songs that fade away, quickly and swiftly hymns will remain. Do things that are not just beneficial to your generation, but rather the unborn, implement an idea that reaches eternity.

257

Wherever you find yourself - in public, private or your personal office - the best thing you can really offer is service, I mean true service. People can't reach into your heart to know how passionate you are about them, people will not reason along to know how much you want to give, but they will all see the results you offer when you give a selfless sacrifice and service. Even the blind can see it, the deaf can hear it, the dumb can speak about it, and the lame will walk tall in it, once they are emotionally attached to the extraordinary service you provide. Be passionate about all that you do!

258

Clean your own hearts. Clean up your own families, your people, your clan, your friends and everything near you. Leave a legacy behind; live it, like the trumpet sound, loud and clear. And the lives you've touched and the truth you cherished will one day, someday and somehow, heal the wound that wickedness and hatred had brought upon our land!

259

One important thing you should keep in mind as the New Year unfolds and the old year winds up is not to forget your origin; your source of life. Remember, your breathe is owned and controlled by someone; give this person all the attention He deserves.

260

You should not be afraid when retrenchment looms, when the hammers are raised and when the blast of the terrible one comes like a storm against the wall. You are a covenant child!

261

Beware of friends that are wolves, but are in sheep's clothing. You can only know a true friend if, searching through his actions and deeds and the book of his heart, you are on the same page with him. True friends are friends that stay with you though every other person condemn your actions and outcomes. True friends always stay put.

262

You will always triumph over every situation that appears tough, troublesome and tempestuous, especially when you long to see the end from the beginning!

263

As we move towards the end of the year, ignite the thoughts of peace, grace and favour and cling unto God's implicit faith, all the things that needed to give way for your miracle to unfold will surely do so as quickly as the flash of an eyelid!

264

Expect nothing or less from people, be positive about them. People will and may always fail, but the principles and virtues of God will and can never fail!

265

Cherish the value and beauty to live in peace and unity. You will attract unrest, chaos, disunity and fear when you allow people that are envious and people who scorn the virtues of truth into your core!

266

What if you're asked to quit your job today? What if someone delays your salary tomorrow? What if...? We need to create a "what if" situation in our minds, so we can plan how to make "if" with what we have. Be always prepared for a "what if" situation!

267

Don't hesitate to put all you've got. When we put all we've got (our strengths) to achieve a major and a highly competitive assignment, all we need is a tone of the supernatural; the invincible hand that turns the tide of favour to our paths!

268

Sometimes it seems you can't even continue. You are down with discouragement, doubts and fear; and you want to quit. You feel like saying goodbye to the routines and the stress when it seems all is falling apart; you need to be careful, because there will always be a reason to look for the things that will stand upright; there will always be a reason to be patient, a reason to wait, just a little more!

269

When you open up your mind, you open up your thoughts, you open up your heart; I can assure you that your mouth will automatically open up. BELIEVE in yourself.

270

From the abundance of the heart, the mouth speaks. Let the words that come from your mouth be ultimately seasoned. Let them not cut through the heart nor pierce through the flesh! Weigh your words so dearly; you never know how far they can travel either to make alive or kill alive!

271

Some people think that living anyhow is the best way to live in mastering the art of living, people who live anyhow; secure anyhow results, but those who live by the rules often see the end from the beginning!

272

*Remain always in the midst of the optimist
and the people that will rekindle hope in you.
Pessimists will drag you down the ladder of success
and kill your dreams. Pessimists are already down
and they need people to join them on the ground floor
of failure.*

273

*It's not hard to know people that have a clean heart
and a clean spirit. Everything about them comes
out so clean that they always look out for the best in
other people. Their hands are never soaked in blood.
When they sleep, clean spirits watch over them and
they spend their nights in clean thoughts and rest. A
dirty heart attracts evil and death.*

274

*Be a symbol of joy and gladness! Create light
from within to tarnish darkness from without.
Laughter is just another way for people to know how
sweet or bitter you are from within!*

275

*Look, leap, lean and learn the art of excitement. Let
it spring from your heart. Learn to go all the way
to make a way for the best in others. Love starts by
giving; does not mean you empty your bank account
for someone; it starts by considering other people, by
giving your little*

276

*N*ever say hurtful things to a weakened heart.
Sing the songs of peace to a joyful heart. Ignite
happiness in the one everyone calls sorrowful, create
life in the dying soul, prepare food for the hungry,
clothe the naked life...these are the reasons why you
are living in these times.

277

*T*he passion for excellence, the desire for
genuineness, the aura of greatness, the hands of
love, the words of encouragement, the plethora of
humility, the heat that banish cold, the water that
kills thirst, the hope that chases fear, the togetherness
that increases faith - are the ten candle lights that
must not go off until you complete your journey in
this life.

278

*L*earn to suppress your anger and ultimately
forgive and forget. This simple virtue of life is a
healing tonic for a wounded heart!

279

*W*e may not be aware nor even imagine how
it feels or looks - 100 thousand people said to
have died in the Haiti earthquake in a suppressed
atmosphere of mourning, tears, fears and death in the
same world where things are rosy, cozy and exciting
for some others. What an irony of life! Remember life
is always in two faces.

280

Scientists predicted some years ago that some people are living on the hot zones of the world. Their warning was ignored; all of a sudden, the grounds are opening up and swallowing humans alive. A city once marked with tall buildings is now left in rumbles. So exasperating and so painful. But who is to blame? Mother earth? Dreams have been killed, visions dimmed, hopes shattered, and all and all are gone too soon and so soon! We should always heed warnings; warnings are signpost designed to either stop us or to make us continue.

281

Imagine how it feels when you give all you have – your money, your time, your effort – to someone, who never appreciated your tenderness and the kindness. You are just being reminded that whatever belongs to the children, never, and I say never, give it to the dogs!

282

Your parents are like a treasure valued above every other treasures; your parents should be honoured, respected and adorned. They are the minds that saw the YOU in the vision; you are their dream come through!

283

*A*bility to do what is right at the right time in the right place and with the right people does not mean everything will always be right!

284

*M*ake sure you wake up early, early enough to do something that will draw you closer to your goals. Just as bathing is mandatory, and brushing our teeth protects us from tooth decay, so also that one thing that will make a big difference in your life! Happy goals year!

285

*H*ave you taken your dreams to the land where it will never grow old? Take your goals by the hand and let each day mark something you can tick out. As you stroll in, walk through and run out of each month, make sure you're achieving something!

286

*Y*ou will always need God to go before you to paralyze everything designed to stand against your success and your glorious future.

287

Whenever you wake up from a deep inspiring slumber, act upon the drops and words of life, and the thoughts that awaken unending desire to breakthrough. They are unborn greatness conceived in your spiritual womb crying to live life. You need to give them a chance. You must start acting upon them, because you will regret going to the grave with them. I pray you recognize these thoughts when they come knocking through the walls.

288

Don't try to be a local champion, be an international champion. In fact, be an intercontinental star - a real man is the one whose impact is felt among people of every tribe, every tongue, and every age; a man whose imprint is inscribed on a platter of gold that is enduring through generations, and transcending all kinds of prejudice!

289

Like the river flows everyday and remember her course, so men should live everyday and don't forget what events played out the previous day. How often do you remember in bits all you did each and every day?

290

Ideas conceived bring forth innovations congealed. Always remember that there is no innovation that human history has ever recorded without first being conceived in the hearts of men as simple as ideas!

291

When you don't write it down, there is every likelihood that you would forget it, every possibility that you wouldn't do it. Cultivate the habit of reflecting and documenting all you'll achieve each day, so get a diary and have a to-do list!

292

Imagination is only sensational when imagination is bathed in reality. Don't allow emotional sentiments becloud your sense of reasoning!

293

Stay clear from the envious that disguise as a friend; run as far as you can from a friend who finds it difficult to tell you the truth, even though it could cost him!

294

Y ou will not succeed, learning the art of pleasing
everybody; instead, you will be satisfied and
successful knowing how to love everybody sincerely,
and from your heart.

295

B reakthrough thinking brings forth out breaking
results. When you think the same way, day in
day out, in the same manner, with the same pattern,
people will take you for granted. Nothing new is
coming from you. You are the same old recycled
personality. How far or near you will go depends on
how much works you exert with your brain. Think
differently, the world can give anything no matter
how much it will cost them to any brain that
thinks strategically!

296

S how me a persistent, consistent, tenacious and a
stubborn man, I will show you a satisfied, peaceful
and accomplished man. The world envies people that
are committed, people who exert their energy into
one singular purpose, and one singular cause; they'll
always get there, even to their Eldorado!

297

D on't always judge people by what you see or hear
about them; learn to draw your conclusion from
your interaction with them, although this may
not be enough.

298

*I*t is highly publicized that first impression lasts longer. For how long can first impressions really last? Can it really last to the end? Truth is, last impression can outlast your first impression, so learn to be your best even though it could be your last opportunity.

299

*W*hen you trample and ignore favour, and you treat it as rubbish, it will run away from you. Show me a man struggling with everything, I will tell you how hard it could be when a man is deprived of favour!

300

*D*on't be ashamed of what you have, don't be ashamed of who you are, because that's not where you really will end your life. You did not create yourself, you did no create where you are, but you can recreate who you are and where you want to be. Appreciate the you that is in you.

301

*G*o the extra mile, do a little bit more, add more value, make all the difference, and stretch yourself slightly further, then when other contestants are getting the ordinary award, you'll get an extraordinary reward.

302

*B*e free, the continuous assumption that you're being watched is a weapon that can deter you from achieving peak performance. Forget the audience and do it well as though you are alone in your living room where no other eyes are watching.

303

*A*lmost all the rivers on earth runs into the sea - be it the Atlantic, the Pacific or the Indian ocean, - they never get filled. Enlarge yourself so much that no matter who runs into you or no matter what is taken from you. Ensure you have enough space and make yourself much more than enough. Never go dry.

304

*B*uild yourself an empire of knowledge so when people ask you about what you stand for in your occupation and vocation, you'll always have answers for them. You have been given the opportunity to create the excitement about what you know.

305

*D*on't live everyday in the hope that night and day will never cease. Understand that you are mortal, and like the day or night you will cease to exist one day. So live everyday to the full, live everyday in immaculate satisfaction. Then you can whisper boldly: "now I can say goodbye"

306

The delicacy of a great meal and the freshness of a cold drink are appreciated by those who are hungry and thirsty. The sick barely bothers about food or drink, neither are those on life support. If you are alive and well, never cease to say thank you to God all the time.

307

Learn to be calm; learn to sit back and observe. Don't ever rush out like others do; don't ever rush in like others want to. Learn to be patient; you never know if there is a great dish in front swallowing hasty hearts!

308

The people we love - our family, our friends, our neighbor - won't always be around us. We need to cultivate new friendship in a new environment. How far we'll feel the bond we had with our past will determine how near we'll feel the warmth of the people in our present.

309

Always believe in yourself; always trust what you can do. There is always a way out for those who believe in the strength of their faith, and their Godly inspired gifts.

310

*D*on't destroy your foundation; don't ignore your beginning. The things that bring you to the top, the effort that makes you stand tall and remain on top will always keep you up there. You have to cherish these things no matter how little; you have to keep doing them.

311

A man who stops dreaming, who stops hoping, who stops trying and have given up on hope is like a cow tied down to be used for meat instead of being used for producing milk. A man who stops aspiring for new things is dead while he's still alive. Don't be like this man.

312

*D*on't speak rashly, don't utter words in anger. Your words are like seeds, when they touch the ground, they'll germinate. Learn to keep your tongue and speak seasoned words even though you are angry. Great wars of words, great weapons of words are enough to cause a national disagreement.

313

*R*espect and honour are like brothers and sisters, when you respect yourself and other people, you will be rewarded with the same. Certain doors would remain opened when your life is governed by respect and honour for other people.

314

*J*ust know what you want out of life, don't follow
the band wagon. When you choose your own way,
the world may reject it, ridicule you, and ignore
you. But endeavor to stay on! When you eventually
succeed, the world will celebrate you.

315

*I*t is compulsory that the human body rest
everyday; it must lie there unconscious in the
dark and at night. You imagine the same body that
is active during the day, very active, is now inactive
regaining lost strength. Just like our own bodies need
this retreat, we also need to exercise our hearts to
consciously retreat our minds to ultimately return
with so much vigor and renewed wisdom.

316

*S*o many waters may have passed under the
bridges; so many people slept in good health and
woke up paralyzed; so many dreams started and
could not endure the wars of the deep nights; so many
camel may have prepared for the journey, but could
not scale the dryness of the desert; so many battles
may have been fought and were lost before it was
dawn. In the midst of the odds, I am grateful that I
have life. I am delighted to say THANK-YOU-GOD
for today, what about you?.

317

*D*o not dwell too long on the victory of yesterday; strategize for today, so you can secure a spot in tomorrow's victory. Leaving the past behind will help you focus on what you have to do today to make tomorrow a lasting victory.

318

*S*o many creatures seem to be in a hopeless situation: they kill or are being killed. Some await the unforeseen to sweep them into their grave, and their spirit goes down and beyond. But humans have been created in the image of the creator to have dominion, so humans are creators too. Tragically though, many people live their lives on the same assumption and reality of mere animals. What a paradox!

319

*I*gnorance is toxic; don't live your life like a fool.
See beyond the vision of mortals. See far into the
future. The less you talk, the less you argue; the less
you eat, the less you hate; the more you pray, the
more you're quiet; the more you read, the more you
enrich your power of observation. These virtues
empower the depth and strength of your knowledge
for success.

320

$\mathcal{Y}$ou don't need to proclaim your greatness by noise and fanfare. Great men are identified by the tenacity of their presence.

321

$\mathcal{D}$on't bother yourself about people who laugh with you, yet want you to fail. Never mind enemies that disguise as friends, yet are ravenous wolves in sheep's clothing. They are always there to make you stronger. If you will get to the top; if you will break records; if your name will be the sweet flavor in every man's lips; you must not be perturbed by the number of people that dislike you.

323

$\mathcal{F}$riends please engage your mind with the people who for sure really long to love you. These are the people that really matter - their words of hope; their plethora of humility, their wings of care, their sweetened and refreshing water of life; their presence that spring up joy; their silent altitude of glory and glamour; their hands held high in victory all being veritable sources of joy and hope. Remember them whenever it seems you're surrounded by people who don't really care.

324

R eal love does not have conditionality! Learn to love genuinely and unconditionally!

325

N o one is above mistakes! Mistakes are usually caused by poor judgment, carelessness, low reasoning and insufficient knowledge. When there is an error, you need to be calm. You need to resort to your back-up plan. Learn a lesson from Akio Toyoda's Toyota Company that recalled about 8.5 million hybrids, hi-tech and highly scrutinized branded cars back to the factory. Was this a mistake or a makeup?

326

U ncontrolled isolation is the mother of loneliness, while self destruction and laziness are from the same family. It is not good to allow the wicked one toil with your innocence, your being alone. Connect, network, associate, socialize, relate, and integrate – these fellowships and the likes we all need to get to the top!

327

C haracter is like flames, no matter how long you hide it or cover it in pretence; all it requires is just one event unknown; it will burst into open anger! A standard ethical value from you will build your character, and when you value other people like yourself, you'll have succeeded in molding your personality.

329

"The Principles of Adeatology", is all about everyday thoughts; it's all about reasoning; it's all about living right; doing the right thing at the right time, it's all about reality. We are not always right in life, but life will always be right.

330

The measure of a truly great man is not in the number of resources he can gather, but the numbers of people he is able to gather with his resources; the number of the sick he gave sound health; the number of the hungry he fed; the number of destitute he was able to provide for! How close are you to becoming a great man?

331

Many of the things we run and crave after don't really matter in the true sense - they are ephemeral temporal and like the chaff the wind will blow away. Give more time to those things that gladden your heart; things that will always spring joy in your soul. Invest your time and money on things of greater value than things of lesser value.

332

There is no mountain you cannot climb! Man has gone beyond the tallest mountains of the world, beyond the supposed boundaries of the earth, landing on the moon. Today, many are exploring mountains beyond life realities, climbing higher into mountains unknown, unexplored and untapped so don't be afraid! You can overcome!

333

The costliest metals in the world, the most expensive resources in the universe are not located on the surface; they are drawn deep, very deep and far into the subsurface. You are far from being outstanding if you don't have depth!

334

Make sure whatever you are doing today, you premeditated the outcome, they will either spare or hunt you in the nearest future; learn to live today as if tomorrow is a shadow, always trailing you and its being carried all along and on your shoulder!

335

You won't know who God is, by not learning about him, when you know him, you'll fear him, when you fear him, you will understand the basics about living, dying, the physical and the spiritual; He showing you awesome things beyond human reasoning you will be stunned, I can assure you, riches and honour will run after you and grab you.

336

You can be easily pulled up by someone who's already on the top. When you stay with a bottom bound individual, you can be dragged down so easily.

337

L earn to spend less; learn to give more; learn to save more; learn to live life; learn to do things accordingly, orderly and with caution.

338

N ever fail to scream the truth! Your voice may not always be heard at the top, your plea may not always count among the crowd, but your worth, your actions will someday remind them that you fought hard against their ignorance yet they ignored you.

339

D on't be envious of him who eventually gets the prize, because the one who gets the prize has already paid the price! To get the price therefore you'll have to pay the price, you must give what it takes.

340

O nly those that start a race will either think of stopping along the way or finishing at the touch line. Those who never start at all, who always think of when they'll be in the race, do not belong to any category and do not deserve any reward!

341

Smart people are neither slow nor fast; they are patient, careful and willingly take interest in letting go. With patience and care you will achieve more with minimum error. When you are in haste you achieve less with maximum error.

342

It's easier to speak the truth than tell lies. Your peace will outsmart the river's when your heart is saturated with nothing but an unending desire to always speak the truth in all your ways!

343

When you live an unapproachable life, it inflates your ego and makes you feel your status have increased also. Truth is, your ignorance has just only increased. People you ignore around you will likely see dangers you cannot see, how would they inform you if you are not approachable?

344

You have to develop and find joy in the things that take over 50% of your existing time, what I mean by existing is the time that you are not asleep. Learn to ignite yourself, learn to enjoy yourself, learn to delight yourself, learn to glow in the things that occupy most of the time you'll be spending here.

345

When you learn to protect things that belong to other people, if they find out, they will love you, they will cherish you, they'll promote you, and they'll do everything that matters to you, because now you also belong to them. I tell you they will not hesitate to trust you with everything.

346

Mercy and truth are like husband and wife - they go hand in hand. When you are truthful, mercy will never cease in your life. It will always come back to you like a ball thrown against the wall. It is a boomerang. When you throw mercy at others they will retaliate with truth, and vice versa.

347

When men praise you, never dwell on their words and their tongue, you never know what is in the bottom of their hearts. They may praise you with their tongue, but their hearts are full of envy, discord, hatred and gross animosity. People watch and I say watch everyone who showers you with praise.

348

You need to be consistent, never appear and disappear like the rain does when it falls. An inconsistent man will always produce inconsistent results; people who do not stick to a particular outcome will never have any good result attributed to them.

349

*A*lways seek to help other people achieve their goals, never swallow stones of hatred when your neighbor succeeds or shouts for joy. Remember to always have a reason to rejoice with people that have something to celebrate, success reproduces success and your glory may likely depend on the story other people have to tell. The glory of the moon is the sun. Not until astronauts returned from the moon, I never knew the moon was so dark!

350

*P*ray when all is well, remember to pray when all things seems to be cozy and rosy, you never know the unseen battles ready to swallow you up, and your prayers will go before you to make a way out of every upcoming troubles.

351

*L*ife is all about a journey, no matter how far, there will always be an end. Activities of today are there to ensure we complete our journey here; no matter how much we engage in them, they will always come to an end.

352

*G*ood personality is contagious, when your personality reflects excellence and exceptionality, people around you will catch the flame. Like a flammable element they'll ignite what you reflect and you'll be very happy to realize your footsteps have now become paths others long to thread!

353

Getting to where you really desired and where you've always aspired to reach will only take a gradual process. You need to see the end from the beginning, but don't ignore the little things you'll do to get there. The truth is many little things come together to make bigger things.

354

A "people person" is someone who always finds a reason to appreciate a fellow human, be it small or great. When you are weak, you need someone to make you strong; when you are down, you need someone to raise you up. When you're alone you need someone to be with you, but you'll never get this someone to come around when you are not a "people person!"

355

You will never go wrong when you ignore someone who is ready to argue and have a fight with you. He spreads his lips, he curses, and he's battle ready to make you realize that his strength is always there for him. Please ignore this person; such people are like powder that scatters in the presence of the weakest wind and are forgotten so easily.

356

The world is no longer a big place; it is now located in your mind, in your heart and even right in your house. You don't necessarily have to be in a particular part of the world for your dreams to come true. Use what you have today to bring the world closer to you, to get what you want.

357

I have never seen a man who stands for something and was never tempted, persecuted and rubbished by the ignorance embedded in the hearts of men. Never known anyone with a strong will and passion for a particular cause; a man that stand out among so many, whose choices were not so openly accused, and questioned. If you are not abused openly or not ignored systematically, you are yet to start any significant thing that will bring about the change you want to see, not any significant thing that the world can attach to you.

358

If I was a..., I would have done that, if I was with this, I would have achieved those, and with who you are, what have you done so far? Use what you have to get what you want, use what you are to achieve what you yearn and long for. The creator created you to complete specific tasks on his creation!

359

So many things are out there that can turn your
life around: some of them are even in there, lying
dormant in your brain, sleeping unperturbed in your
mind, walking languidly in your heart. These great
ideas are lying fallow and begging you to utilize them
so your name will fly high among great achievers, but
you'll never know them if you find it difficult to make
wisdom your best friend!

360

*I*t is not how long the body stays here that matters, but how well we use our body to make long lasting and enduring impact; and also how well we use all the resources that are attached to the body - our mouths, our eyes, our hearts and our voices. Let's utilize them to channel hope and love unto all men.

361

*Y*our thoughts about certain issues are not necessarily the same as what other people feel and think about the same thing. They probably had forgotten about it. Don't dwell so much about what people say or think about you, dwell so much on what you say or think about yourself.

362

*T*he greatest reconstruction of all time is change - change is dynamic and fascinating. The most important change is the change you want to see. Imagine a situation whereby someone you know to be evil, unfriendly, secluded; whom you thought is living with the virus of wickedness in his blood stream; suddenly turns around to be friendly, loving and attractive. The ancient words of life squeezed out the truth in him and melt his stony heart who can explain this change? - The potent power of words can facilitate unimaginable transformation.

363

L *eadership and authority belong to those who live in the future and who can see them in the picture of their imagination. People who live in the present are controlled by the present, they are ignorant of what comes next, and they are vulnerable to any unforeseen, unannounced and sudden circumstances. People who dwell on the past are shallow, less realistic and unadventurous. For those who see the future, major breakthroughs are sighted a far, and are embraced. The minds that conceived the future live uncompromisingly for what they've seen. See the future beyond today!*

364

T *here is a popular saying that "you don't put the cart before the horse". I will advice you not to use the cart at all. When you combine the cart with the horse, you will be stuck between two decisions to put the horse before the cart or put the cart before the horse; save yourself this headache and use the horse alone. You would have minimized wastage and distributed effort efficiently when you concentrate your decision intelligence on one particular direction.*

365

*I*n my research and search for God, I discovered
something fascinating and explainable. Anything
unrighteous, everything ungodly, all things done
in deception can never be from God. Everyone who
practices things that are wrong cannot be from God.
You can now see clearly that the principles of this life
that leads to excellence are from the unfailing
laws of the almighty.

366

*F*rom the deepest part of the deepest ocean beyond
greater depths to the highest clouds where rain
drops, and from the tallest mountains ever climbed
or unexplored, and the lowest valley or depression
ever known or seen, man will always be in charge
of everything. The power inside a man can only
be harnessed by those who either physically or
spiritually has ever traveled thus far. There is a
powerful force residing in the inside of you, explore it,
allow it, refine and extract it for the glory of God!

So every one that will come across these principles, as long as they read them, will all live a more structured life, they all don't need to agree with me but they all who finds something captivating and worth actualizing in these words, will understand that somewhere and somehow, someone has written something, to make sure they never leave their dominance unknowingly.